T0418323

Dedicated to my beautiful children
Maya and Kai. It brings me immense joy
to see you both celebrate
and embrace all your cultures.
Your blended beauty
is only half the reason you are
beautiful, your kind soul is the other.
I love you more than love.

To my Nieces, Nephews,
God, and Dream Children.
You will always be loved and cherished by me.

Tia Bua is so excited to share that our family is mixed, blended, colored and rare.

We all come from different parts of the world too
and we speak different languages
yes, it's true!

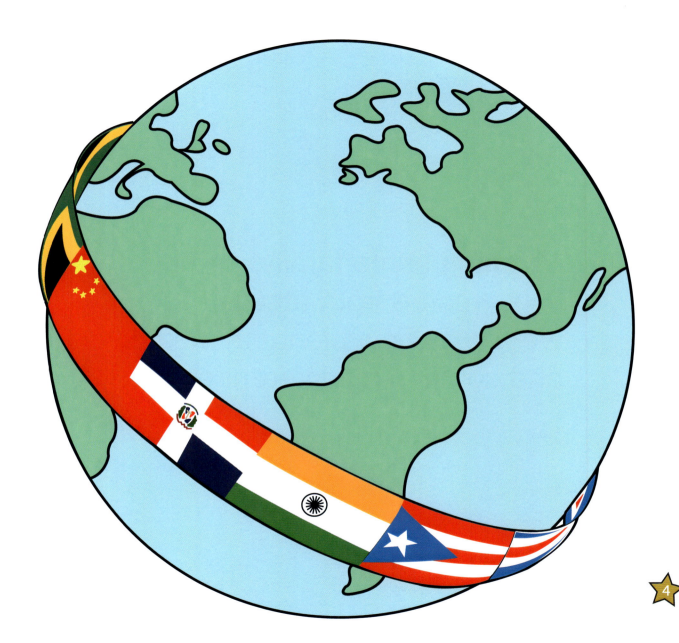

Although some family members
came from others,
we are all now blended, mixed,
and come in all different colors.

Tia Bua loves when her family comes
over to laugh and play,
so she invites everyone over
to have a very special day.

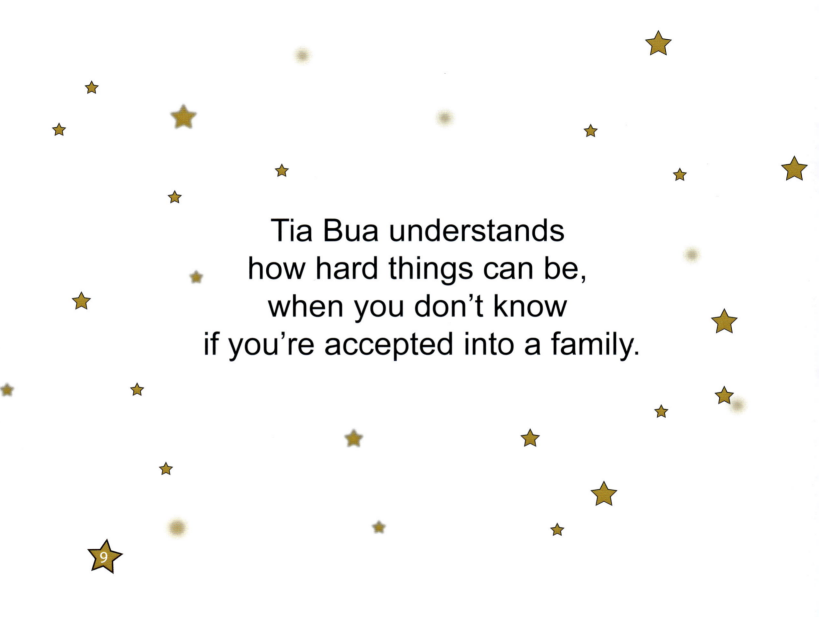

Tia Bua understands
how hard things can be,
when you don't know
if you're accepted into a family.

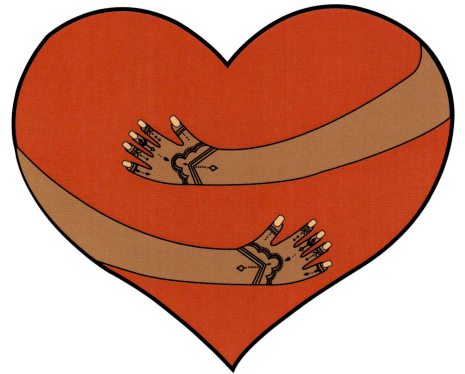

That's why her favorite dish to serve
is a house full of love,
with it wrapping around everyone,
just like a hug.

With food from around the world
and everyone coming from near and far,
Tia Bua invites her family
to come just as they are.

She believes you make this family whole
because you have a kind,
pure, and beautiful soul.

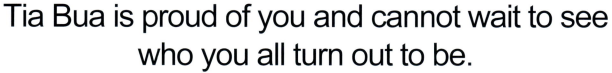

Tia Bua is proud of you and cannot wait to see who you all turn out to be.

When things get hard remember
to close your eyes
and take deep breaths of three.

Then whisper, "The magic is inside of me."

1- Breathe in the magic…Release the magic.

2- Breathe in the magic…Release the magic.

3- Breathe in the magic…Release the magic.

Let your magic set you free and whisper,

"The magic is inside of me".

See it does not matter where you come from, what you look like, or who you choose to love. Tia Bua believes you were sent to this family from the stars up above.

Your heart should always remain kind and true,
Always remember Tia Bua loves you!
The End

Acknowledgements:
Maya Santiago
Vivek Desai
Kai Desai
Aalyana Santiago
Dayana De Pena
Darius A Hicks Sr.

Nico Desai